Indescribable Hurt

NAVIGATING MY CHILD'S SUICIDE

- By Eileen P. Brymer

When my daughter ended her life so unexpectedly, I needed to empty my brain which was continues to overflow with questions. My story chronicles the confusion and disbelief surrounding the enormous grief that I have had to learn to live with.

TABLE OF CONTENTS

Introduction i
Chapter 1 – The Shock 1
Chapter 2 – My Intuition 7
Chapter 3 – The Funeral Service 17
Chapter 4 – Guidance and Support 25
Chapter 5 – Taking The Blame 31
Chapter 6 – Rules, Laws, Mistrust! 39
Chapter 7 – The Guilt 49
Chapter 8 – The Unrest 55
Chapter 9 – Trying to Understand 59
Chapter 10 – Second Guesses 65
Chapter 11 – The Holidays 71
Chapter 12 – Looking for Signs 76
Chapter 13 – The Medium 84
Chapter 14 – Grieving 89
Chapter 15 – Present Day 95
Epilogue

If you suffer great loss, it's never going to be okay. It just will never, ever, be okay. It is part of the grain of who you are, and it is then embedded in you for the rest of your life.

INTRODUCTION

April 19, 2014 proved to be the worst day of my entire life. No event that I perceived to be worrisome or disastrous before or since that date can compare to the horror. My only child, my Colleen, took her own life. Sleep will never be the same and upon waking, I will always feel like someone has punched me in the chest. I will spend every waking minute trying to answer the question "why?"

Colleen was a beautiful baby, of course, and would grow up to be a beautiful woman. She had smooth peaches and cream skin, beautiful blue eyes, and long, fine, silky red hair. She looked quite a bit like me, and had a few of my northern character traits. Although I grew up in New York, Colleen was born a "Georgia peach". I used to call her "mini-me," taking license from the Austin Powers movies. Colleen's smile was contagious to anyone who knew her. The last time I saw that smile was two weeks before Easter. We made plans to see the movie "*Noah*" and have dinner at her favorite Italian restaurant. I don't know if my memory only believes what I want it to believe. I remember that visit as one of the best we ever had. We liked the movie, luckily, and had a scrumptious meal. My grief hits every time I think of that day and the tears flow again.

The tears come unexpectedly. I never know when they will surface. It has been over a year since Colleen died, but it feels like yesterday. My father died in 1996 and I have had numerous conversations with my mother about grief. I never understood hers, but now I do! Trying to compare the two life-changing events is futile. No one person's grief is the same. It did not make me feel better to hear that this grief would be with me for the rest of my life. Granted, it may not continue to be as intense, but the loss of one's child is indescribable.

I couldn't believe how fast the business of an autopsy and the arrangements for a funeral move. Colleen was here, then she was gone, removed from her apartment, sent to the medical examiner, autopsied, cremated and buried within 5 or 6 days. There were too many questions and financial concerns to address. I must have been in shock; how else could I have sat there and picked out an urn as if I was ordering cookware from a catalog? As I write this, I wonder, where was Colleen? Surely her spirit couldn't have left that fast. It would be many months before Colleen's spirit found me in my sleep.

CHAPTER 1

THE SHOCK

I'm awake but I don't want to open my eyes. The pressure in my chest reminds me that Colleen is not here anymore. *Oh my God, did she really kill herself? Is Colleen really gone?* As soon as these thoughts enter my head, my day begins. I want to go back to sleep so I don't have to feel anything, but, Daisy, my Shih Tzu, is doing her dance, telling me she needs to be let outside for her morning bathroom ritual. I have to get up.

I suppose it is a blessing to have Daisy, or I'd never get out of bed. Once I start moving, the memory replays as if Colleen's death had occurred yesterday. The sun is shining through all the windows and doors of my simple ranch style house in the country, so I should be happy, but I'm not. I am unable to envision happiness in the days ahead.

I don't understand how I can sit here and contemplate the chores that need to be done, when the realization that Colleen killed herself slams me in the chest with such force, as if somebody punched the air out of my lungs. I am paralyzed until I can breathe again. I talk to myself and plan all I need to accomplish, but I am unable to get myself moving.

After my father died, whenever I'd go home to visit, I would envision my father at the store or at work. Even though I knew he was dead, he was not really gone to me. After Colleen passed, there was nowhere I could go and just assume she was somewhere else. When I went to Colleen's apartment immediately after her passing, I felt that I was violating her privacy. I could pretend she was at work, but the same process that worked for me after my Dad passed did not work this time. Dad was older and sickly, but Colleen was young and vibrant.

I still can't believe she's gone forever.

I would enter Colleen's apartment, expecting her to greet me. Instead, the shock of what had happened throttled me again and again. I would go into her bedroom and stare at the spot where the police found her. Not receiving a response to any of my phone calls, emails, or texts for several days, I had alerted them to perform a welfare check. I thought maybe she had fallen and couldn't get to her phone. I was not permitted to enter Colleen's apartment until after she had been taken to the morgue, so I only had the images in my mind that I created. It all felt so unreal. I wanted to come out of my fog and find her smiling at me. Colleen always told me I worried too much and that I was silly. I wanted her to tell me that again. As I sifted through her belongings, more than once, I stopped to ask Colleen something. Shock ensued! She would never be able to speak to me again!

I have this urge to scream at the top of my lungs. The burning in my chest from holding back is excruciating.

The subject of suicide is generally not talked about, unless it pertains to a celebrity or a discussion surrounding a documentary or movie. When it becomes the subject of your life or that of an immediate family member, you really do need to talk about it.

Your family and friends do not want to talk about it.

I would repeat the word "suicide" so I could get used to it. It *is* a horrible word! I can tell you that repeating "suicide" to yourself will not help you get rid of the shock. I tried other phrases, such as, "took her own life," or "ended her life," but those words didn't carry the same conviction. "Passed away" did not sound plausible. People did not understand "passed away." Colleen was too young and had not been ill. Everyone seemed to want and need further explanation. Rather than having to repeatedly explain how Colleen died, I put "suicide" front and center.

You could see the shock on their faces. How did this happen? I won't say it happened to me, but it did happen to an extension of me. Colleen was a part of me! She was my only child, my only daughter, my life!

Then you have the stupid people. I remember when I went to the bank to close Colleen's account. I handed the bank employee her death certificate, my power of attorney and other necessary papers. I wasn't prepared for the bank employee to be clueless. He stated that Colleen had to appear in person to close the account, and continued to ask "why does she want to close the account?" I'm sure I looked like a wild animal as I strangled the words out of my mouth, *"Because she's dead!"* Granted, my emotional state was questionable at this time. Silence blanketed the bank and the proper procedures were followed. I had assumed that once you told someone that a person was dead that they would know what to say or how to react. I was expecting too much from people in the state I was in. I know I continued to experience the shock repeatedly during the months following her death. Two years later, when I think about it, it continues to shock me – not so much her dying, but how she died.

CHAPTER 2

MY INTUITION

In January of 2014, I fractured my right arm in three places. I had gotten a new Shih Tzu puppy and the little girl managed to get under my feet causing my downfall. I needed help, but as I am an independent person, asking for help was foreign to me. Performing day-to-day activities without one limb is extremely burdensome. Although off balance, and loopy on painkillers, at the time, I was and am blessed with wonderful friends. I lived almost an hour away from Colleen in Temple, Georgia. As she had her job to attend to in Atlanta, I knew it would be impossible for her to take two months leave to be my right arm. As luck would have it, my neighbor's sister had moved to Georgia and was looking for work. I hired her to be my caregiver. It was a blessing!

I thought Colleen would be relieved, but I was disturbed to read Colleen's emails after her death. It's difficult to ascertain a person's real feelings in electronic communications, but she seemed angry and upset with me.

Colleen, because I didn't ask you to take off from work, did you think I didn't need you? I would have loved for you to be with me, but I was trying to be considerate and not make your life more difficult. I hope now you understand, albeit too late.

Colleen did visit me in the hospital, during an ice storm no less, and came to the house to help me on the weekends. She had told me, "Mom, if you need me, I will be here." So when I was having guests at my home for Easter, I told her I needed her.

Colleen told her peers at work that I wanted her to come for the weekend. She ended her life two days before Easter.

Why, Colleen? What was the catalyst that made you forget about your plans and your life? We could have talked a lot while you were with me that weekend. I never judged you, or berated you for any decisions you made. Why would you feel I wouldn't understand now?

I was on the mend, having had two surgeries on my arm; one in February, and one in March. I hadn't received a response to my texts, emails or phone calls from Colleen for about four days. I was redecorating my spare bedroom in anticipation of her visit. I wanted to know her preferences regarding pillow type (hard, soft, etc.), when she would be arriving, and other mundane questions. I was excited about seeing her. When I didn't receive a response by the Friday before Easter, I began to get agitated. I assumed Colleen was busy at work trying to finish up projects so she would not have to think about work all weekend.

Saturday arrived and I was doing as much of the preparation for Sunday as I could with my broken arm. But where was Colleen?

Something was wrong. I called her girlfriend to find out if she knew where Colleen was. She said, "don't you know?"

Know what? I knew nothing! Only then did I find out that she was in a battle for her life, and had quit her job two weeks earlier. Why didn't anyone feel the need to break confidences and let someone in her family know what was going on with Colleen? I don't understand that. If one of my friends or family was exhibiting unusual, out-of-character signs of dangerous behavior, I would speak up! Who cares if they got angry with me! I'd rather lose a friend over doing something to help, than lose a friend because I did nothing!

As soon as her "friend" told me Colleen was in trouble, I hung up the phone and called the local police for a welfare check on my daughter. I also called my sister; who lived 15 minutes away from Colleen. I asked my sister to call me in my car once she was at the apartment. During the drive to Colleen's apartment, I heard nothing from my sister. My body turned ice cold. I knew it would not be good news. I just didn't know how horrible it would be.

The weather was sunny and clear as I drove through the apartment complex with the cookie cutter buildings. As I pulled into the parking spot next to Colleen's car, I didn't see my sister or anyone in distress. The detectives and crime scene investigators appeared so calm. They must be immune to death because of what they see on a regular basis. When one detective told me, Colleen was gone, I asked, "what hospital did they take her to? What happened?" He explained that "gone" meant "dead." I was not ready for that. It was incomprehensible to me.

At first, I was stunned. The questions commenced. I remember yelling and crying when I heard she had left a note. The fact that Colleen left a note removed any doubt that it was suicide. I wouldn't accept that. I couldn't believe it. All I can think of was *"what??"* To make matters worse, the detective wouldn't let me see the note! I assume because the crime scene investigators were taking it as evidence. The detective would only tell me what it said, but I was skeptical. I wouldn't believe it until I saw it. When I finally did see a copy of it at the police station, it didn't help at all. It did not provide any clues. It did not alleviate any of my pain.

I remember my sister calling my family, but I don't remember much of what was said. There were a lot of questions being asked. Did Colleen have mental problems? Of course not! A little depression, maybe, but no *mental* problems! When did I speak to her last? What made me call the police? I had to sit go in my car as my legs started to crumble beneath me.

Even as I write this, I don't know how I ever found the strength to go up to her apartment after the detectives, crime scene investigator and medical examiner departed. Yes, crime scene investigator! They confiscated all pharmacy bottles, the note, and anything else they needed for their reports. The authorities distracted me while they removed Colleen from her apartment. I was so angry because I wanted to see her, hold her and talk to her one last time, but I wasn't allowed.

Even as I viewed her bedroom where the deed had taken place, it wasn't real to me. I don't remember how I got home that day. I am angry at myself to this day for calling the police. If I had just gone over there myself, and found her, I would have had one last chance to see her. Who knows, I probably would have tried to revive her or wake her up. At least, I could have held her.

"If only" will be the beginning of every thought and sentence for me for quite some time. My family and friends have stated that it would not have been good for me to see her. How do they know that? They don't. It might have made more sense to me, if I had been able to see or hold her. I was never told how long she had been "gone" before we found her.

Because I was prevented from seeing her before the authorities took her away, I have my own version of the scene created in my mind. When did she take the pills? How many did she take? How soon after she took them did she become ill? She was found on the floor of her bedroom, after attempting to get out of bed. Was she trying to change her mind?

Every day since that day, my imagined sequence of events play in my mind over and over in a continuous loop. I create alternate scenes; one, where I am able to find her before she succumbs to the effects of the drugs. I help her into the bathroom and clean her up. I walk her around her apartment to keep her awake. I watch TV shows where they do that while waiting for the ambulance to arrive.

Another alternate scene is where I find her and she's on the floor, but, at least, I am able to hold her and tell her I love her, but my vision of these scenarios does not stop the flow of tears and anguish. They only enhance my quest for "what if?" I feel that if I were able to hold her or see her, it would make it more real. Seeing Colleen in the coffin did nothing for me. It was not her.

After going to the medical examiner to discuss their findings, going to the police department to obtain copies of her suicide note, and making several trips to the courthouse to file for probate, it was a matter of waiting. I mean, waiting, waiting and waiting. When a person dies from a drug overdose, it's the toxicology tests that take forever. Once the toxicology report is completed, the standard wait time is 90 days for the death certificate to be administered. You can't do anything with a person's estate until you have that death certificate.

CHAPTER 3

THE FUNERAL SERVICE

The slideshow of Colleen played at her service sent me over the edge. I had no idea I could experience this much pain. It squeezes your chest and attempts to stop your breathing. It makes you cry out, and it doesn't change a thing. I had to interact with all the people in my life who knew about Colleen and with whoever passed through Colleen's life. It was standing room only.

I must have acted like a lunatic at Colleen's service. One minute I was sane and the next minute I couldn't remember why I was there. I felt like I was at a surprise party attended by people I hadn't seen in years. There were so many people that there was a "receiving" line I thought would never end. I know at one point I was trying to get someone to go up and see Colleen. I was horrified that I was doing that! Why would I do that when **I** didn't like looking at Colleen in the coffin? I realized afterwards that some people don't want to see the body in the coffin. They prefer to remember the person as they were in life. I already knew that, but for some reason, I wasn't thinking straight that day. (Sarcasm added.)

Nothing seemed to go right. The funeral director who was our contact was out sick, so someone we had not worked with was taking over. As a result, our requests were not filled. The music wasn't loud enough. The eulogies were too short.

In months to come, as I relived the service over and over, I had an intense yearning to get up there and speak. Of course, that was just irrational. I couldn't have spoken a word coherently.

I wanted everyone to know what a wonderful person she was, how funny, how talented, how smart! I wanted to tell funny stories no one had heard. These are thoughts that come to mind after it is all over.

How did we pull this all together so quickly? Colleen's father (my ex) assisted, along with other family members. When someone dies, the disposal of that person is completed in days. You don't have time to think, much less make such important decisions. Funeral directors are quick to steer you through the maze, but there really is no time. Yet in hindsight, none of those issues seem important at all. I think that two, maybe three years down the road, when some of the pain has subsided, there should be a party to celebrate the person. During those years, everyone has time to gather memories, stories, and mementos that were meaningful and happy. As it is, the process happens so fast that only the first and foremost in your thoughts is conveyed. The sorrow, sadness, and grief are so overwhelming that they overshadow the best of a person's life – at least it was that way for me. You see, if Colleen had died in a car accident or of natural causes, I would surely grieve, but not like this. It's the manner of her death – suicide – that is out of the ordinary. I could handle losing her, but not this way.

There was a beautiful little girl, with long curly blonde hair, who came up to me. I say "little girl" because I still thought of Colleen and her girlfriends as "little girls". They were someone's children and grown women. This little girl was consumed with grief and could not stop crying. She couldn't speak. All I could do was hold her, and try to get her to calm down-everything I couldn't do for myself. I never got her name, but that image has stayed with me. This girl was exhibiting what I was feeling. I couldn't let it all out. I had to stay in control and take care of business.

"Colleen, can you see everyone's sadness? Do you see how you left has affected all of these people?" It wasn't the real you who left us. You were not in your right mind. Those damn drugs! They altered your mindset. I can accept you were in pain. We all have our struggles in life. That's why we lean on family and friends during hard times. The drugs gave you an easy way out. You thought it was an easy way out. It wasn't, was it?"

When my Dad passed away of heart disease at the age of 71, my mother gave the funeral home a photo. The funeral home made my Dad look like he was 40 again. They did a fantastic job. The funeral home did not ask for a photo of Colleen, and I didn't think to provide one.

I did not like the way Colleen looked in the casket. It really did not look like her. Her peaches 'n' cream skin was dark and sallow. Her beautiful red hair was dark and stringy. Her arms were purple. Later, I read somewhere that antidepressants can change a person's skin color. If I had known that, I would not have picked a short sleeve blouse to dress her in. In any event, I really did not feel that Colleen was there. I was so used to seeing her smile; seeing her in that state was so far from what Colleen was really like. The essence of her was gone. It took all my restraint not to grab onto her, lift her up and hold her. I was deprived of that and, for me, it was palpable. I was in agony. Everything was being crushed inside me. The urge to scream had returned! Being an adult, knowing how to act in certain circumstances, really inhibited my true emotions. I'm sure if I let loose, they would have put me in a straightjacket and had me committed. Those emotions would have to wait.

As it was, I reacted loudly when the minister couldn't pronounce Colleen's name correctly. I shouted, "it's Col-leen (soft 'o'), not "Coe-leen". When I named her, I didn't know what a problem it would pose for people to pronounce. Colleen had asked me once if she could be called by her middle name instead. *Colleen, was that a clue that you didn't like yourself? Lots of people don't like their names and use nicknames or middle names.* "Andrea" never stuck. Colleen was definitively a "Colleen," which means "Irish Lass."

I watch or listen to Billy Graham, Joel Osteen and other spiritual programs. One day I heard it said that the second year of a loved one's death is worse than the first year. I find that to be true. Emotionally, I was numb. It all felt so surreal. I would wake up every day and I would say to myself "No, that didn't happen. Colleen's not gone. It can't be!" Then, once again, reality sets in. I did not see my daughter in the casket. It was only what was left of her. I did not feel her spirit. She was gone! Just like that – poof! How do I comfort all of these grieving people? Everyone was as devastated as I was. *Colleen, are you sorry you left us?*

After everyone had filed out of the chapel, I went up to the casket one more time to say goodbye. Little did I know that the wheels on the casket carrier were not locked. I faltered and leaned a little too hard on the casket. It moved! If there was ever a time that I would die of heart failure, that was it! I thought I was knocking it over! I could hear Colleen saying *"Only you would do that, Mom!" Colleen, if I could have you back, you could make fun of me all you wanted to.*

CHAPTER 4

GUIDANCE AND SUPPORT

Colleen's apartment complex was beautiful. The grounds were meticulously kept and the clubhouse overlooked a lake with a park-like setting. It was the perfect place to sit and contemplate, especially on a warm, sunny Georgia day. To ask questions. What had happened? Why didn't she call me or her father for help? Why didn't she call any one of my brothers and sisters? Someone would have helped her. I sounded like a broken record.

Colleen, there was so much beauty around you? Why did you feel so isolated?

Colleen had a support system. She had five aunts and three uncles in my family alone. Although they lived in New York, someone would have listened to her. Her father and his family lived in Georgia and North Carolina, in close proximity for her if she needed help. My sister and I lived close by. She had a best friend, but I was told Colleen wouldn't even open up to her.

What was so terrible, Colleen, that you couldn't tell anyone? During her mental breakdown in March, one month before she took her life, she told her office manager that she didn't want anyone calling her parents. She didn't want to disappoint us. I am still floored by that! It wasn't like Colleen had never confided in me.

Colleen, I helped you through surgery, job loss, love lost, and financial problems. Why didn't you know that I would help you through whatever was happening this time?

My intuition failed me miserably. I ponder all the practical reasons that could have contributed to her depression; that is, lack of love life, job pressures, or financial woes. In essence, it could have been all of those things exacerbated by the drugs. Those god-awful drugs! We're talking about legally prescribed drugs, not street drugs! Colleen was under the care of professionals, doctors who had prescribed Lamictal, Cymbalta, Wellbutrin, Abilify, Ambien and others at various times and in various dosages. Upon researching these drugs, I was horrified at the list of possible side effects, both major and minor. Any one of them cites a whole host of problems that can occur, including but not limited to, depression, sleepiness, anxiety, and can cause suicide. They were treating her depression with drugs that can cause depression.

Needless to say, my faith was taking a hit during all of this. I have always believed in God, angels, and spirits. I tried to raise Colleen by teaching her about prayer and having Jesus to rely on in times of trouble. She received her First Holy Communion and her Confirmation. I know none of these things is proof positive that someone believes, but Colleen told me she believed in God and I believed Colleen.

This demon was stronger than she could handle.

 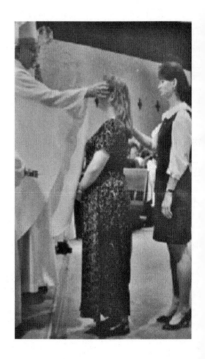

Colleen's suicide envelopes my world in a gray shroud.

Upon entering the apartment, not only did I feel that Colleen had died, the apartment itself felt dead. I know the apartment is an inanimate object and objects don't feel, but all feeling had left the apartment. Colleen told me she believed in God. In her apartment, "FAITH" "HOPE" and "LOVE" plaques are on her wall. Going through her jewelry, I found a necklace, charms and keychains with "HOPE". "HOPE" was on her Facebook page. "HOPE" was everywhere. *Colleen, did you know that "FAITH" and "LOVE" are equally important in life? The greatest of these is "LOVE!" So many people loved you! Any one of us would have helped you.*

I am looking for clues everywhere that might tell me "why?" Colleen left a note saying *"I'm sorry. I love you, Mom and Dad."* Every time I think of that note, I get angry all over again.

Colleen, did you ask God for help? Did you really love us? How could you sit there and write the note knowing that you would be negatively impacting so many lives?

A normal human being of sound mind wouldn't have sunk so deep. I cannot bring myself to believe that the person writing the note was Colleen. It wasn't her. She had to be under the influence of the legally prescribed narcotics!

CHAPTER 5

TAKING THE BLAME

To reach Colleen's apartment required walking up three flights of stairs. Having health issues, I avoided going there for that reason. Now I wish I had gone over there more often and suffered the discomfort of having to take those steps. If I had, I might have seen the deterioration of her living conditions.

Whenever I had been there in the past, it was homey, lived in, not excessively neat, but there was no clutter in the living room; the guest bathroom was neat and clean; the kitchen was in order. Now, I was dismayed at the appearance of chaos. Dirty clothes everywhere, under the kitchen table, on the sofa, on the floor of her bedroom; there was no room to walk around in her apartment. The kitchen sink was piled high with dishes; the counters were cluttered with bottles of alcohol; the ashtrays piled high with cigarette butts. The guest room that I had stayed in on several occasions looked like it had been ransacked. I was beyond shocked! It was blatantly obvious that Colleen had been struggling for some time. I blame myself for not being able to see that she was in trouble.

Throughout her life, I believe we had some great times. Over the years, we made numerous trips up north where my family lived.

On one of our trips to New York City in the late 80's, Colleen and I, along with some friends I've known since the '60's, and their children, visited FAO Schwartz. Always the prankster, Colleen was just the right height to get a pat on the head from the life-size polar bear. FAO Schwartz closed July 15, 2015. Time passes quickly.

One of her high school band trips was to New York in April 1996. I consider it one of the highlights of Colleen's life, but I wonder if I enjoyed her life more than she did. Colleen was the light of my life! *Colleen, I hope you knew that!*

When she was 8, we went to California to visit a friend of mine who had a son Colleen's age. We went to Disneyland! Colleen loved Disney! She would visit Disney World in Florida several times over the years!

She enjoyed traveling on occasion with her aunts, whether it was to Ruby Falls,

Tennessee, Orlando, Florida, Myrtle Beach, South Carolina, or Hershey, Pennsylvania.

When Colleen finished school and began her working career, we traveled to San Juan, Puerto Rico, for the Thanksgiving holiday. We stayed at Rio Mar, rented a car and went to the Bacardi factory, where we sampled different flavored rums and vodkas. It was one of many wonderful adventures. Colleen introduced me to mojitos!

I wonder if a person can have a "midlife" crisis at 30s. I organized a birthday trip for Colleen to the Inner Harbor, Baltimore, where her aunts from New York surprised her. She was so happy and excited. We all have a wonderful memory of that time. When I attempted to piece together Colleen's life and where it went sideways, it appears that after that birthday, her life began to be troubled.

We traveled to Nashville in 2011 and 2012 to attend the Country Music Four-Day Festival held each year. She loved country music as much as I did, and we Colleen had her photo taken with Mark Wills. We had a blast. I didn't know at that time Colleen's health was already beginning to decline. There were NO signs. Did I miss the signs? Was I not present? Was I too wrapped up in myself that I didn't see? We went to Gatlinburg, Tennessee for Christmas 2012, and I still didn't see! Only after I found the receipts for the filled prescriptions did I know that she had started to have problems in 2010. The drugs were supposed to help!

They say that mothers can always sense when something is off with their children. When Colleen helped me celebrate my 60th birthday in 2011, it was the best birthday celebration I had ever had. She had decorated her guest room for me in 60's streamers and banners, and the usual birthday party hats and balloons. My sister, Colleen and I went to Dave & Buster's and had the best time. Dave & Buster's is a combination restaurant and arcade, such as you would find in an amusement park. We laughed so much! There was no indication of depression, or any change in her personality. If anything, Colleen was very loving and happy celebrating with me. I blame myself for not being more perceptive. But maybe that day just happened to be one of her "good" days.

CHAPTER 6

RULES, LAWS, MISTRUST!

I can only search for answers by talking to the people who were in her daily life. The hearsay is that, about a month prior to her death, Colleen, hysterically, had approached a co-worker stating she was having thoughts of killing herself. Immediately, the supervisor took her to the mental hospital and Colleen voluntarily checked herself in. Colleen sat with her supervisor for almost ten hours talking about "things". At the end of the day, the doctors decided Colleen was no longer a danger to herself or others. How can they deduce that?

If anyone had contacted me, I would have been there with her. If I couldn't have her committed, I, at least, would have stayed by her side indefinitely. I would have delved into the drugs she was taking and what was turning my daughter into someone I didn't know. The excuses I have been given for no one contacting me are irrelevant and meaningless to me. Through this whole ordeal, I'm told that HIPAA privacy rules prohibited her employer from contacting family. My anger is palpable!

I believe the medical examiner, the psychiatrist, her general practitioner, the doctor in the mental hospital and HIPAA all failed Colleen miserably. I feel they didn't do their jobs. The doctor in the mental hospital knew Colleen was in trouble when Colleen stated she was thinking about taking her own life. After admitting her, they waited all day and watched her. At the end of the day, they believed she was no longer a threat to herself so they let her sign out. I am incredulous! It bears repeating! If I had been there, that would not have happened! How can a person overcome suicidal thoughts in eight hours?

Because Colleen had not signed any release waivers for anyone, not her job, not the doctors, they were bound by HIPAA laws and could not call me. I strongly believe there should be exceptions to the HIPAA laws! The psychiatrist (and those in the medical group) should have been monitoring Colleen, but with the evidence I found in Colleen's receipts of her visits and prescriptions, what stood out was that her prescriptions were changing all the time. I believe they gave her too many prescription drugs at the same time. Colleen did not sign a waiver for her information to be released to anyone. Again, the psychiatrist was also bound by HIPAA laws and could not tell me what was discussed in Colleen's sessions, if anything.

Colleen, I am haunted with not knowing what was troubling you. Why didn't you sign the waivers? You can't be embarrassed by what I'd find out, because you are gone. At least I'd have some answers. You were worried about us finding out something about you that you considered so terrible. I wonder how you think we feel now?!

The medical examiner's report had a few errors in it that I could not explain. It stated Colleen's gallbladder was intact. What? Colleen had her gallbladder taken out in June 2011, and I was there for the surgery. If the medical examiner could make such a blatant mistake, it made me wonder if they had the right body. What other mistakes were made? Was the toxicology report correct? I trusted no one.

Hindsight is always the best. I should never have had Colleen cremated. I could have exhumed her body for further investigation. I consulted a lawyer, who sent Colleen's records to a professional prescription drug attorney. I wanted to sue somebody. Upon review of Colleen's toxicology report, medical examiner's report, and autopsy, the drug attorney ascertained that no one was at fault, except Colleen, of course. I was, irrationally, searching for a mitigating cause of Colleen's death. True or not, I will always believe that the doctors are at fault. If you read the inserts to any of these anti-depressants, they all cite "suicide" as a possible side effect. If you prescribe 3 or more anti-depressants to one person, surely the risk of suicide is multiplied.

The inserts also state that if you notice a change in behavior or have thoughts of suicide, you should consult your physician. REALLY? If you live alone and you are depressed, and no one is around to notice a decline in your habits or demeanor, how can you, a sick person, report yourself? I'd heard that people suffering from depression are good at hiding their true feelings. I wish I didn't have to find out firsthand , but now I know that to be true. I would see her every couple of weeks. She would be immaculately dressed, manicured, and polished. Colleen was beautiful and smiling. These are not signs of depression. I had no clue! I am told that my feelings about any perceived negligence on the part of the medical profession are, understandably, "emotional," but there is nothing I can do "legally."

Depression should not be fatal! When a person is an alcoholic and they attend AA meetings, they are provided a sponsor, someone they can call at a moment's notice if they are in trouble. Here you have professionals dispensing lethal "legal" drugs with no supervision! If you have a family or are living with someone, there is a better chance of a change in behavior being noticed. However, if you live alone and are in crisis, and don't know how to call out for help, someone should be checking up on your regularly. Doctors should not dispense these potentially fatal drugs unless the person can be admitted to a hospital under supervision. Or they should amend the HIPAA rules to make it mandatory that the person seeking assistance gives HIPAA the right to notify a friend or family member.

Colleen went to the mental hospital in March 2014. I had more than an entire month to turn things around for her. No one gave me the chance and now it's too late! I'm looking for someone to blame. I can't bring myself to blame Colleen, so it's easy to blame myself.

I sound like a lunatic myself. I'm crazed about this broken system.

I don't remember what prompted the discussion, but one day in 2012, while taking a drive, Colleen told me that she was "getting help" for her depression.

I knew about the depression. Over the years, she and I had talked about her need for therapy due to a particularly bad romantic breakup. I thought that she was blocked from having a new relationship and that some therapy might be in order. She would tell me she didn't have the funds. Eventually, Colleen had received a welcoming increase in salary, so now she could afford to pay for the sessions. I was ecstatic that she was beginning therapy! What Colleen didn't tell me was that she was seeing a psychiatrist, not a psychologist.

What's the difference? A psychologist cannot administer drugs. They offer talk therapy. Psychiatrists do too, but if the patient doesn't want to talk, there are always the drugs! Colleen opted for the drugs. I gave the "professionals" the benefit of the doubt. I thought they knew what they were doing. Now I believe the system is broken and I blame them!

At that time, I did not press for details because what she discussed with her therapist is her business. I did wonder if she would ask – or the therapist would request – that I attend a session with her. That never happened. She proceeded to tell me that she had been prescribed two antidepressants. I was familiar with these drugs. They are advertised daily on television. Colleen was an adult so I *thought* she would make the right choices for herself. At the least, I *thought* she would consult me if she had a question. But maybe it was I who should have asked more questions. I tried to do that once in a text message, but Colleen emphatically texted back, "I'm getting help and NO I don't want to talk about it." That's where the conversation ended. She didn't offer any more insight into how the therapy and drugs were progressing, and I wished her the best.

I didn't know what else to say. I told her I was there if she needed to talk. It was up to Colleen if she wanted to go into more detail. She may not have talked to me about everyday life, but had always come to me with the more complicated issues. We always worked them out together. Her being prescribed drugs didn't alert me to the fact that she was seeing a psychiatrist and not a therapist. I should have known! The drugs were changing her. The guilt is back! Do I need another reason to berate myself for not seeing the signs?

CHAPTER 7

THE GUILT

Very quickly, I realize my life will never be normal again. An abundance of conflicting emotions consume me. In 2012, after working in Washington, D.C. and living in Virginia for eleven years, I returned to Georgia where it all began for Colleen. My gorgeous redheaded little girl was so glad to have her mother back home again – or so I thought. Of course, she wasn't little anymore. In her early thirties, Colleen was now a single, successful business woman with a life of her own.

When I started making my plans to buy my home, I presented several scenarios to her. Since she was renting, I thought, maybe, she would be amenable to my buying a duplex or a two-family house, so we could be close and available to help each other. Colleen's reaction or non-reaction to my suggestions became obvious to me. Unrealistically, I expected our relationship to pick up right where we left off 11 years earlier. While she and I were glued to the hip when she was younger, that tie had been broken. She no longer wanted to live with me. I assumed she wanted her privacy and I respected that. I backed away and gave her space – maybe too much space. It was my fault. It was easier for me to blame myself. I felt I deserved all the pain I was feeling. I'm stubborn.

It took a long time and, finally, several visits to a grief counselor to talk me out of it.

Colleen's place of employment was five minutes from her apartment. I would drive there and take her and her friends to lunch. Those were happy times and I hang on to those memories. A cake for her birthday, cupcakes for Valentine's Day, and cookies for Halloween would magically appear on Colleen's desk on their appointed dates for Colleen's enjoyment. I thought these treats would break the monotony of the daily grind. I believe it's the little things in life that matter the most.

I tried to maintain contact in any way I could. We didn't see each other enough for my liking. I would call or text Colleen regularly and was agitated when I didn't receive a response. When I did receive an answer, she would be angry with me, or so it seemed. It's hard to tell with technology; emotions are not easily identified. Colleen would text, "I'm busy!"

I know how it is to be immersed in one's job. I didn't know why Colleen could not take a minute or two out of her day or week to send me a message. All I needed was *"Hi, Mom. Just checking in. Busy here at work. Talk to you soon."* Was that too much to ask? We had this argument several times. I realize now that when someone is ill, even a simple task as sending an email becomes a chore. Why couldn't I see that then?

I feel guilty for thinking about what I needed.

I feel guilty for my failure as a mother to see her child was in trouble.

I feel guilty, I feel guilty, I feel guilty ….

Will it ever stop?

Catholic guilt is not a myth. It's very real. My friends try to comfort me by telling me there was no way I could have known what was wrong with Colleen. She wasn't forthcoming with her thoughts and feelings. I rationalize that I couldn't read her mind. That is small consolation. Colleen's still gone. It would be almost two years for me to come to terms that it wasn't my fault. The "what ifs" plague me.

What if:

- I hadn't gotten divorced when she was a year old.
- I hadn't moved us around so much.
- I hadn't worked so much.
- I had expected too much of her.
- I hadn't left Georgia.
- I had forced her to talk more about her therapy.

I can keep going.

The adage, "time heals all wounds," is not true. It does take time for the different stages of grief to play out. There is no schedule. Everyone's timetable is unique to their situation. I had to keep living day-by-day and address each thought as it rambled through my brain, until I found a satisfactory place to stop feeling guilty. You can talk to friends, family, and others in a similar situation, but no one can stop your feelings for you. People in my life repeatedly suggested that I see a therapist. I knew better. I could handle this on my own. Besides, my guilt told me I deserve to suffer.

CHAPTER 8

THE UNREST

I lay awake at night thinking about Colleen. My mind replays the imaginary film created by the events of that April day. Sometimes I re-create the way I wished it had happened. I want to be the one who found her. I want to save her. When the detective told me "she's gone", I wanted it to mean "to the hospital" – not that she died. All re-creations are futile attempts to change the outcome and try to fall asleep. The burning in my chest begins again in my attempt to keep from sobbing. Some nights it's 4 a.m. and I'm still awake. I pray *"Colleen, where are you? Please send me a sign. Help me sleep!"*

My mind relives Colleen's entire life searching for clues. My thoughts go back to the time when Colleen was an only child and we lived together until her senior year in high school. Her father and I divorced when she was a year old. I would never take Colleen away from her father, so her parents were always living in close proximity of each other. I would always tell her how much she was loved. A child needs to hear it, as well as feel it! I was a hugger; Colleen was not. I am a crier; Colleen was not – at least not in front of me. Colleen hated to see me cry, and I did my share. Being a single parent had its ups and downs, to say the least. I tried to raise Colleen in every way my parents didn't. I think, *"Colleen, I'm so sorry. What went wrong for you to take your own life?"*

I wonder whether I said the right things to Colleen. It is too easy to fixate on what I perceive I did wrong. I find it difficult to remember the good things I did for Colleen. I did find a message I had written to her in 2012. I cherish it, and whenever I start doubting myself, I read the message. It reminds me that I did tell her I loved her, that I did want her to be happy, and that she did make me happy.

It really makes no sense to dredge up anything that was said or done in the past. I cannot change anything, cannot undo any wrong. I am continually wondering what was going through her head. My poor child! She had to be going through terrible anguish to feel there was no help for her.

I don't know how I was able to perform everyday functions, but I lost my mind very fast, and it is taking a long time to come back. I went through everyday life in a haze. As time passes, my mind seems to find a place to settle and it stays there. Some days I still have trouble making simple decisions. It depends on how I slept the night before and how I feel when I awake. I have trouble deciding whether it's worth it to do simple tasks, such as whether to take a shower or to make breakfast. Many days I end up in front of thse TV for hours. I'm getting better. It really helps to have something to do planned for the day. Yet, through all that has happened, I have still managed to perform the responsibilities connected with owning a home, paying bills, and taking care of my dog, Daisy. As I write this, I ponder how in the world I've managed to do that. Only time will tell if I made some silly or stupid decisions during that time. I don't remember!

CHAPTER 9

TRYING TO UNDERSTAND

Not only because Colleen passed on, but also before she died, I would cry every time I browsed through her baby pictures. Every new parent is told to cherish those early years because the time passes very quickly. That is not a cliché. If you were to browse through the albums of photographs I have taken of Colleen through the years, you would see one happy child. She was smiling all the time.

As a baby, Colleen was cared for in a Kinder Care day care center while I was at work. Colleen knew my schedule like an alarm clock. At 6:30 p.m., she would be standing in her crib with her arms held wide, as I came through the door to pick her up. I can feel that love to this day. Of course, it makes me cry, but everything about Colleen makes me cry now. As a photographer, I know that a photograph can mask the real emotions a person is feeling at the time the photo is taken. I can continue to enjoy the genuine expressions I see on my baby's face in all the early photos.

This is a photo of Colleen, about 5-6 years of age, taken in an Olan Mills professional studio. Years later, she would tell me how much she hated that haircut and photograph. I love this photo! At that early age, Colleen had started keeping her true emotions to herself. You can't tell from the expression on her face that she's unhappy.

Colleen and I had a memorable visit during a calm, balmy, autumn night in 1998, when she was attending college in north

Georgia. We were taking a leisurely walk around campus, when she told me she was smoking cigarettes and drinking beer. Smoking and drinking beer was the least of my worries. In my mind, drugs and casual sex were far worse. Colleen commented that she was surprised that I didn't over-react, and that I wasn't disappointed or judgmental. I told her that she was now an adult and had to make her own choices. We talked about the medical ramifications of smoking and how she felt after drinking beer. We laughed because I happen to like beer, but Colleen hated it! I would find out later that she loved rum and vodka!

The years flew by. After a year, Colleen left college and started working. She eventually found her niche at a privately held physician services company. Wherever Colleen worked, she excelled. Colleen would tell me that she was so glad that I had instilled in her a good work ethic. *"Oh my goodness, I did something right!"* To an outsider, her life was no different than anyone else's life. Her boss, Joel, will tell you how valuable she was to him. Colleen moved up the ranks to become a "Director" with a good salary.

At times, she had financial problems, but nothing that couldn't be fixed. I know she lamented the school loans that plague a lot of young people for years after they've finished college. I had no facts to warn me that Colleen was unable to handle anything that life handed her. When she was young, she stated, on several occasions, that she did not want to grow up. I'd laugh it off because I think we all felt that way at times, but it was inevitable and unavoidable!

I never took her comment seriously. Maybe I should have. I had weathered too many trials and tribulations in my life not to believe that she could too. I taught myself how to get through life, but Colleen had me! I was always there! Maybe it wasn't financial troubles that Colleen was depressed about.

Colleen, I wish you were here to straighten everything out for me!

I remember when Colleen turned 28, I informed her that, at her age, I was married and was giving birth to her. Colleen was horrified and made it perfectly clear that she would never have children. I didn't believe her. Some women say that, but when the perfect time presents itself, they change their mind. Maybe I should have taken her remark seriously.

"Colleen, what could possibly have happened in your life that was so horrific that you had to end it?"

CHAPTER 10

SECOND GUESSES

My brain is on overload. Living alone, retired, not having additional family members to take care of, no job, and no routine to keep me busy, leaves a lot of time to think. I'm second guessing every decision I made after Colleen graduated high school. Up until that point, Colleen and I did everything together.

In 1996, I took a job offer in New York, but before I did so, I sat her down and we talked about how it would affect her. If she didn't want me to go, I would *not* go. She was in her senior year in high school, but she was never home. Her social life was full. She had her driver's license and a car her friends had dubbed "the tank." It was an Oldsmobile Cutlass that held all four of her girlfriends. They went everywhere together. Mom wasn't needed anymore for pickups and deliveries. I could trust Colleen to be where she said she would be and to call, if there was ever a change in plans.

Colleen was a good child. She was an A student, first chair in oboe and flute in the marching band, and was never in trouble with the law. I was very blessed.

In 1996, I was offered a promotion, but I'd have to move to New York. Since Colleen was entering her senior year of high school, she was a busy girl and was never home. After discussing it with me, Colleen told me to go to New York and I did from July '96 until March '98 when I returned to Georgia. While I was gone, she would live with her father, enabling her to stay in the Conyers, Georgia school district and finish her senior year. I returned to visit several times, including attending her special band award ceremony, and her high school graduation in '97.

Upon graduation, Colleen went away to college in northwest Georgia and was on her way to creating her own life. Although I went through severe separation anxiety when I moved to New York, I really enjoyed returning to Georgia for visits and being with her during the high school award ceremony. When it came time to move her into her dorm, it was a wonderful experience for both of us. Since Colleen never showed her emotions, I tried to keep mine in check. I sobbed all the way home from the college, but thought her college experience was a positive step in her growing up. I knew she would have to carve out her own niche in life and I couldn't tag along anymore. I needed to give her wings.

I wondered how Colleen felt. She would often mock me for my sensitive emotions. I was shocked and dismayed when I learned many years later, how sad she was when I left. I never knew; she never told me how she felt. She never cried when I left for New York. *Was this a major mistake? Colleen, did you need me and I deserted you? I'm so sorry!*

In 2012, when there was no way I could rectify the situation, she would tell me how she cried every time I left, but she didn't want me to see her crying. She said she didn't want to stop me from having my career and enjoying my life. I felt like I had been stabbed. This broke my heart! She held her feelings close to her chest. How do other introverts cope? If I had to be an introvert, my insides would explode. I am the exact opposite. Everyone knows what I'm feeling because I display my emotions openly.

I returned to Georgia in 1998. Colleen left college in 1999 and she moved back home with me. She started a serious relationship, and they were talking marriage. In November 2000, I had another opportunity to relocate, this time to Washington, D.C. Colleen and her future husband would live in my house. It was the perfect arrangement. I didn't have to sell my house and Colleen could have a home and pay a low mortgage, instead of having to find a new place. NOT! After three attempts at planning a wedding, her relationship fizzled two weeks after I relocated to Virginia. Colleen was devastated; the relationship had depleted her. She was now 21 and on her own.

The next 11 years consisted of regular phone calls, emails, vacations, and planned visits to and from Georgia, and Virginia, where I had bought another home. We talked for hours about family, work, social events, and our plans for getting together. I never had a clue that something was not right.

Colleen experienced ups and downs in her life, both when trying to find the perfect job, and making new friendships. We've all been there. These experiences are nothing unique. I even suggested at one point that she come to Virginia. There were numerous colleges to choose from if she wanted to return to school. She could live with me until she completed her degree. I also felt that she would make new friends.

Colleen never took me up on my offer. I didn't tell Colleen that I had decided to go back to college in 2003 at the age of 52. She googled my name for some reason, and an entry came up on the computer, stating that I was on the Dean's List. Colleen told me she thought that, if I could get my degree at my age, then she should go back to college. She subsequently finished her four-year degree.

CHAPTER 11

THE HOLIDAYS

In early September 2015, I awoke one morning to the sound of someone screeching. My heart was beating so fast in my chest. After a few moments, I realized it was ME. Some mornings my pillow is sopping wet. I must cry in my sleep. I was unable to let my emotions flow during the first year following Colleen's death. I had to hold it together in order to complete the innumerable tasks associated with someone dying. To this day, I continue to relive Colleen's passing--over and over again.

The slightest smell, song, photo, memory, or sight starts the waterfall. I do not sleep well anymore. I used to love the fact that I could sleep anywhere anytime. I never had a problem.

Now, I have trouble falling asleep, and when I do, I do not want to wake up.

My holiday season will never be the same without Colleen. Christmas was Colleen's and my favorite holiday to plan together. It made us giddy with excitement and we acted like kids. It did not matter that we were mother and daughter. At times, we did not feel the age gap. Maybe because I was silly and liked to wear antlers, sing songs, and not be a stuffy old fogey.

Until Christmas Day in 2014, I did not feel Colleen's spirit around me. That was a difficult holiday for me. Many people told me I should not be alone, but I disagreed. I did not want to drag my family and friends down with my presence at their gatherings. I do not know how to fake being happy, and no holiday, vacation, or celebration will ever be the same. I planned a trip for myself to Eufala, Alabama, someplace low key, not too far to travel, and someplace where I had never visited. I don't know why I thought I could escape from my feelings by going away. I wanted to do something different that wouldn't remind me of what it would have been like if Colleen was with me.

Built up tears flowed the entire Christmas day. I went to Eufala thinking the town would be abuzz with holiday spirit and people, but the town was empty of people and did not have any festivities on Christmas. I left a day earlier than planned to return home. Suffering from physical and emotional exhaustion from the drive, that night, for the very first time, I dreamed of Colleen! She was laughing and surrounded by a group of people. That's all I remember. It was enough!

I woke up feeling happy. I interpreted the dream to mean that she was at peace and happy. My sister told me she thought Colleen had seen how distraught I was, and had to comfort me.

Whatever the reason, I was glad, but it was short-lived. The dreams have stopped.

Christmas 2015 is approaching, and this will be the second Christmas without Colleen. I can no longer bring myself to be with people during the holidays. It takes too much out of me to put on a happy face, when I am not feeling happy. Colleen was a very funny and playful person. We spent Christmas 2012 in Gatlinburg, Tennessee. It was cold in our cabin up in the mountains, but we went shopping in town and had a blast.

Colleen purchased this wool hat that sent us into fits of laughter. Colleen looked like an old-fashioned Dutch girl; all she needed were the wooden shoes. She asked me to add the caption, so she could show her friends, but I have no idea what it means. As I look at the photo, I remember and my laughter turns into rivers of tears. Christmas 2013 was our last holiday together and we spent it at my sister's house. I have one last photo of the three of us, but they made me promise not to show anyone because they were in their pajamas and had no makeup on. How trivial that seems now! It does not matter. It is locked away in my memory, along with 34 years of Colleen's life.

Oh Colleen, I love you and miss you so much!

CHAPTER 12

LOOKING FOR SIGNS

Family and friends would tell me how much she loved me. I still have trouble believing that. If Colleen loved me so much, she had to have known that if she left, and in the manner in which she did leave, I would be devastated. If that love was so strong, why don't I feel her spirit?

"Colleen, do you see how angry I am? Is that why you stay away? Please send me a sign!"

I considered Colleen's name to be fairly unusual, simply because you did not hear it or see it often. Since her death, I see her name in odd places. There is a commercial for the new "Watch", where a man looks at his wrist to see who is calling and

I see the name "Colleen." It's inconspicuous and not in any way important to the commercial, but I see it. There will be other signs, but never enough for me.

I was visiting a New York restaurant with friends and the atmosphere was quiet and serene. Out of the blue, someone calls out loudly "Colleen"! Even if you are skeptical about spirits and signs, it was unmistakable that she was trying to let me know she was there with us. We were dumbfounded, and it gave me goosebumps, but it was comforting to me. I'd much rather have her here with me physically. I'm still angry and it makes me cry again!

I hadn't heard from or felt Colleen for quite a while. I gave up on wanting or expecting any kind of sign. I felt that, for whatever reason, Colleen wasn't coming through, at least not in a way that I needed. I had to face that fact.

I think about Colleen every day, but I am beginning to let go. I need to make some progress with regards to having a life again. My photography has taken a back seat. I stay at home too much. I stopped going on weekly jaunts to new locales for photo opportunities. I gave up on losing weight. I had the attitude "why bother?" because nothing seemed to be important anymore.

And then it happened.

I had been dog sitting for a friend. Daisy, my Shih Tzu, enjoys the company, but the dogs get me up at the crack of dawn. I woke up and I tended to their needs. I didn't go back to bed, but fell back asleep on the sofa for a few hours. It was during this nap that I had the most vivid dream. It was a crazy dream as dreams tend to be, because it made no sense. The sensible part of the dream was about my meeting up with people in some town, but I was staying at a different hotel than the others. When I finally arrived at the other hotel, Colleen came out to meet me and I hugged her and kissed her so many times and I wouldn't let go. I kept telling her how much I missed her.

I'm crying as I write this. I could feel her skin as we were cheek-to-cheek. I was hugging her and I could feel her warm body against mine. The feel of her smooth, soft skin and the intensity of my feelings were exactly the same if I were awake.

The shock of the ringing doorbell ended the dream abruptly. Daisy's friend was being picked up. I was fine answering the doorbell and having a short conversation. When my friend left, I remembered the dream and could feel Colleen hugging and kissing me all over again. The impact of those feelings was as strong as the day she died. The avalanche of tears started and I sobbed like never before. I felt those feelings the entire day and I want to keep them with me always. I know those feelings make me cry, but I feel happy at the same time because I love her hugs and the feel of her skin. I do not ever want not to feel them. I want to hang onto them as long as I can.

I had my palm read for the first time when I was in my early 20's. From that point on, I was hooked on palm reading, horoscopes, tarot cards and mediums. For me, those methods of predicting events are fun entertainment. Sometimes things would happen as predicted, but mostly, I had to remember that there were millions of people around the globe with the same horoscope or palm reading. I can pick and choose what to believe and what not to believe.

Having been raised a Catholic, I believe in the Holy Trinity and Guardian Angels. How else could I have survived my life? Believing and having read about how the spirits are always around, I had high expectations that Colleen would visit me regularly. When I did not hear or feel her around me, I began to doubt. My mind started telling me that Colleen was not in a good place because she committed suicide. In the Catholic faith, suicide is definitely frowned upon and if you commit suicide you cannot be buried in consecrated ground.

Because God is an all-forgiving God, I now choose to believe that God has forgiven Colleen. Only He and she know the reasons for her actions, and Colleen's not telling me. Does Colleen feel shame? Is that why she can't or won't come to me? Or am I searching too hard and not letting her come through on her own? I was so anxious to hear from Colleen or feel her spirit.

When my father died, I experienced a small miracle. I was at my mother's house one day trying to install a new doorknob. I have done this many times. For some reason, this doorknob was stubborn and would not line up with the door jam. I was so frustrated. My mother and I were exhausted. Dad was the handyman. So at the same time, Mom and I said "Dad, please fix this doorknob!" and *voila!* It slipped into the groove! I had a similar experience after Colleen died.

I had misplaced a flash drive that I kept in my purse and had torn up my house looking for it. It contained valuable personal information and I would not want it to fall into the wrong hands. I knew it was in the house. I had changed purses several times in the last few months. I searched every purse, every drawer, the desk, and any place where I thought I might have put it down. After two days, I gave up and decided to stop looking. On the second night, I started lighting candles in my living room and sat down to relax. I said to Colleen, "Colleen, please help me find that flash drive." I could not relax until I found it.

I got up, once again, and decided to look in the very first place I had looked two days earlier. It was there! I choose to believe that Colleen answered my plea for help! I read articles, books, and other materials on grief and came across an article on the internet. It was about signs that a deceased loved one is close by.[1] One of the signs is an item being moved from the place you know you left it, only to have the item turn up exactly where you looked the first time. Apparently, your loved one is playing with you. At least I know I'm not crazy!

---

[1] "10 Most Common Signs From Your Deceased Loved Ones," by AmandaLinetteMeder.com (Facebook), January 27, 2014.

CHAPTER 13

THE MEDIUM

Colleen would have been 36 on July 31, 2015. I scheduled a session with a medium on July 30, hoping it was close enough to her birthday to elicit extra spiritual vibes. I was and am agitated that Colleen is not around more often. By this time, I was desperate for some spiritual connection with Colleen. I thought maybe she would come through for me. I wanted to believe so badly. I guess I will have to wait until I die to find out exactly what she is talking about.

The medium described Colleen as a vibrant, bright light. She made me smile and brought me joy. The medium told me that Colleen's scenario was not your typical suicide. This was not the first time I had heard that. I have always believed that there was something amiss in the whole situation.

Colleen had plans. She was in the process of buying a house. She was going to California with her aunts, and was driving up north with me for her uncle's wedding. Also, she was preparing to come to my house for Easter. Does that sound like someone who was contemplating ending their life? They do not make future plans, do they? There is something very wrong with this picture.

The medium said that Colleen had this tremendous pressure building up inside her with regard to depression and addiction. Colleen was "over-indulgent" and had "pushed the envelope too far." She said Colleen had done "it" before, but there were no consequences. Colleen decided to do "it" again.

Colleen's body just popped; she ran out of gas. The medium went on to say that Colleen did not want to hurt anyone.

Too late, Colleen!

She also said that Colleen did not want to end her life; she was trying to find peace.

Colleen!!!! All you had to do was call me!"

The medium commented to me that Colleen needed to tell me *"thank you."* She can breathe and feels more grounded around me. She was restless going to the other side. She had a rough *"end of life."*

That is an understatement!

Colleen had a rough end of life because it didn't go according to her plan. She had taken a copious amount of prescribed drugs. Instead of putting Colleen peacefully to sleep, the prescriptions made her vomit. The vomiting woke her up. Colleen attempted to get out of bed, but because she had taken a sleeping drug, that made her woozy. Losing her balance, she smashed her head into the footboard of the bed and it knocked her out cold. She never came to.

I choose to believe that Colleen had changed her mind. Upon becoming ill, I believe she would have gone to the bathroom and recovered--maybe enough to call me or someone else. Naturally, the "authorities" do not have an opinion on my theory.

The medium continued on stating that Colleen is grateful for my love, and knows that I went out of my way for her. Colleen told her she gave me a run for my money. You can say that again! She said Colleen was proud and tough as nails and became that way because of me.

Was Colleen too proud to admit to her parents that she was sick?

I sobbed during the reading. The burning in my eyes and chest has become a part of my life. Whether you believe in mediums or not, when the medium told me that the "sightings" I had already received were real, it made me feel better. I was not sure that I was making up my small miracles; she gave them credence. The dream and the few times I feel that Colleen is trying to contact me are just not enough for me. The medium did tell me that my grief was a hindrance to my feeling Colleen's presence. She said Colleen is always around me. When time passes on and I begin to grieve less intensely, I will relax and I will feel her presence.

Two years later, I'm still waiting.

Truthfully, I was disappointed. I thought there would be some grand revelation from Colleen about why everything happened. I want to get on with my life in a better frame of mind. But I feel exactly the same as I did before I met with the medium--guilty, unfulfilled, empty, sad, meaningless, and angry! I wonder if I will ever be able to shake the feeling that I am somehow responsible. Occasionally, my Catholic guilt rears it's ugly head, but I have to accept that Colleen's actions were her decision.

CHAPTER 14

GRIEVING

My grieving did not actually begin until months after Colleen was gone. The practical matters that needed taken care of, the disbelief, and the denial interfered with my reaching the point of actual grieving. I didn't see Colleen every day so it was only when I realized I couldn't call her, email her, or make plans to get together, that I realized that she would never be around anymore.

There is no semblance of order to the stages of grief. They do not appear as clearly set out in pamphlets. Sometimes you will experience several feelings at once. I think denial came first for me. Immense anger and sadness came next, but that does not mean these feelings do not reoccur again and again. Depression still hangs around me. I feel a tremendous void in my life that will never be filled.

I cry every time I speak to my mother. She is 91 years old and she cries with me. She wants to help me, but no one can. I start out the conversation promising myself I will not cry, but by the end of the phone call, I am blubbering all over again. I cannot help it; it just comes.

If I do not bring the subject of Colleen into a conversation with my friends, I will not cry. They know if Colleen is mentioned it will set me off. My true friends have been my anchors. They have experienced their own losses in life, but none compares to the loss of a child. I relate to a longtime friend who lost her child as a baby. She is a stronger person than I. Her child has been gone for over 20 years. I am just beginning and I am told I will feel this way for the rest of my life. Not a good feeling!

I will never get the answers I want. I will never know what was going on in Colleen's mind. Colleen cannot help me. It is all about how I am reacting to everything that comes my way that stimulates the memory hormone. The reason why I cannot sleep is because of my obsession over Colleen. The reason I cannot get out of bed once I do fall asleep is because I do not want to wake up and think about Colleen. The reason I cannot eat right and lose weight is because I am trying to fill the hole left by Colleen. The reason I cannot get up off the couch is because I am weighted down with guilt over Colleen. The reason I cannot interact with people the way I used to is because I have changed due to the loss of Colleen.

For about a year and a half, my friends nudged me to find therapy groups or someone to talk to. I finally realized that my friends were suffering when I would cry over the phone. It wasn't fair to them. They felt helpless. I wanted to keep my friends and not drive them away. Finally, I went to see a grief counselor. Faith and prayer can help, but if you are angry at God or are not a believer, a grief counselor can help. I am not into group sessions, so one-on-one was best for me.

My first session was cathartic. I gave myself permission to let go. My heart was breaking and my sobbing was uncontrollable. All the hurt, fear, anger and helplessness came gushing out. Until then, I thought I could handle my loss all on my own. After all, I'm a grown woman and I have weathered life's trials and tribulations up to this point. I can handle one more. But NOT this!

It was only after repetitive insistence on the part of my therapist that I began to accept that Colleen's suicide was not my fault. It was Colleen's decision. Does that mean I am all cured and life will now go on as normal? No, by accepting the fact that it was not my fault, has helped me to try and reclaim my life. At the same time, knowing it wasn't my fault doesn't lessen the pain or emptiness I feel.

CHAPTER 15

PRESENT DAY

When people ask "how are you," how much truth do they really want to hear? Truthfully, I am not doing well. Depression has hit again. What? You thought I was ok now? It has been raining for a week. I am having panic attack s and do not know why. I do not sleep well, so I nap during the day. The Eastern Daylight Time change did not help.

I actually went to call Colleen last night to see if she was watching *The Voice* on TV. I felt so stupid. It started the crying again.

I know this "episode" will pass. I just have to let it play out.

I do not "have to" go anywhere or do anything, so I don't. There is no one in my world anymore since Colleen left. She was my invisible shield. I know I did not always see her, but I knew she was around. Just when I think I am over the shock, I feel so alone. There is no one in the world feeling my feelings. TV is my escape. I find words to express my feelings in everything I see, hear or do. "The same love that lifted you up in life can drag you down in death." (quote from *NCIS: New Orleans*). At times, I feel like I am in an abyss where all my thoughts disappear.

I woke up this morning wondering how many more times I have to do this-- wake up. I do not know what triggers the onset of my depressive episodes but I just have to wait them out. Sadness can render me inactive for days. Then, all of a sudden, one day I am doing well. Maybe depression isn't the correct term

Melancholy or just plain sadness come over me. I never thought that I would have this kind of tragedy in my life.

A very dear friend from NY was coming down for a week so I was making a list of things I have to do, when suddenly the thought "Colleen killed herself" hit like a bolt of lightning. I could not breathe. A neighbor came over for a visit and I was fine, but now I am spiraling down again. Fortunately, my friend will be here a week; someone I've stayed in touch with since we became friends at 13. I know I will be sad when she leaves. I feel like I will be "acting" at being okay for the rest of my life and it's exhausting.

There is no closure to an experience such as this. Gloria Vanderbilt talks about the suicide death of her son, Carter. She said "it demolishes you." I agree. Ms. Vanderbilt looks fantastic, but I know how she feels inside. It stays with you forever. She and her other son, Anderson Cooper, wrote a book about their life.[2] While no one wants to belong to this type of community, it helps to know that we are not alone.

I do know now that Colleen could not handle the pain she was experiencing. Colleen needed to turn off her mind and when alcohol and sleep didn't work, she did what she had to do.

Colleen, I am so sorry you were suffering. I would give anything to have you here with me. You were an amazing daughter and a beautiful person. I hope you are now at peace. I will love you always and forever!

---

[2] "The Rainbow Comes and Goes, A Mother and Son on Life, Love and Loss," by Anderson Cooper and Gloria Vanderbilt

EPILOGUE

I read *Wake Me Up! Love and The Afterlife* by Lyn Ragan. Someone suggested to Lyn that she should write her story about losing her fiancé as part of her healing process. I started writing to Colleen in a journal, and subsequently decided to write my story. My therapist thought this was a wonderful idea. Now, I don't want to stop writing. When I do, I am closing the book on Colleen's life forever. But in my heart I know differently. Her physical life is over, but she is still very much alive in my mind and heart. I could have included hundreds of photographs that chronicled every year of Colleen's life. Upon perusing my photo albums, I realized I had forgotten so much.

This is my story as I experienced it. These are my feelings. No one can tell me that I should feel a certain way, or dispute something I perceived to have happened. Anyone who has a different point of view can write their story.

I was trying to explain to somebody for the millionth time how and why I feel lonely. But I am not alone. I have many people in my life. If someone sees me, there is nothing obvious in my demeanor that would tell you what I experienced. This is true for all of us. In my case, I am lonely inside myself. There is a gap, a void, a space that will never be filled. My emotion stays there and seeps out every so often. No one person in my life can fill that hole. No one can begin to understand how I feel every day. Yet, I keep trying to explain. I was asked by a friend, "Is that important to you? To have everyone understand how you feel?" I guess it is or I wouldn't keep trying. All I can do is pray, seek therapy, live my life, and continue to miss Colleen.

* * *

ABOUT THE AUTHOR

Eileen Brymer, a New York native, is retired and now resides in Temple, Georgia. She has 10 siblings, most of whom still reside in New York. Throughout her career, Eileen held secretarial positions in the government with the FBI and Foreign Service State Department, as well as having been a legal secretary and paralegal in several law firms located in New York, Georgia and Washington, DC. She likes to travel, write, and take photographs. Eileen can be contacted through Facebook, and her photography can be found on the Red Bubble photography website.

Made in the USA
Middletown, DE
08 December 2019